W9-AWL-879

Vermeer

Melody S. Mis

PowerKiDS press.

New York

To Tyler, Emma, Elizabeth and Lauren Raben

Published in 2008 by The Rosen Publishing Group, Inc.
29 East 21st Street, New York, NY 10010

First Edition

Editor: Jennifer Way
Book Design: Greg Tucker
Layout Design: Julio Gil
Photo Researcher: Nicole Pristash

Photo Credits: All background images, p. 6 (top) © Shutterstock.com; cover © Rijksmuseum, Amsterdam/The Bridgeman Art Library International; p. 5 © Staatliche Kunstsammlungen Dresden/The Bridgeman Art Library International; p. 6 (bottom) © Private Collection, Giraudon/The Bridgeman Art Library International; p. 9 © Kunsthistorisches Museum, Vienna/The Bridgeman Art Library International; p. 11 © Metropolitan Museum of Art, New York/The Bridgeman Art Library International; p. 12 (top) © National Gallery, London/The Bridgeman Art Library International; p. 12 (bottom) © Private Collection/The Bridgeman Art Library International; pp. 14–15 © Mauritshuis, The Hague, The Netherlands, Giraudon/The Bridgeman Art Library International; p. 17 © Metropolitan Museum of Art, New York, Giraudon/The Bridgeman Art Library International; p. 18 © Mauritshuis, The Hague, The Netherlands/The Bridgeman Art Library International; p. 21 © National Gallery of Ireland, Dublin/The Bridgeman Art Library International.

Library of Congress Cataloging-in-Publication Data

Mis, Melody S.
    Vermeer / Melody S. Mis. — 1st ed.
        p. cm. — (Meet the artist)
    Includes index.
    ISBN-13: 978-1-4042-3843-5 (library binding)
    ISBN-10: 1-4042-3843-3 (library binding)
    1. Vermeer, Johannes, 1632-1675—Juvenile literature. 2. Painters—Netherlands—Biography—Juvenile literature. I. Title. II. Series.
    ND653.V5M513 2008
    759.9492—dc22

                                    2007010360

Manufactured in the United States of America

CONTENTS

Meet Vermeer

Jan Vermeer was one of the great artists of the Dutch Golden Age. The Dutch Golden Age is the name for a time during the seventeenth century when the Netherlands was a rich and powerful country that was home to many great artists.

Vermeer is known today for showing how light **affects** the colors of objects and how people in a scene look. He liked to paint rooms with light shining through a window on one or two people, often women. These people were doing everyday things, such as reading a letter.

Vermeer painted *Girl at a Window Reading a Letter* around 1657. You can see how light coming in through the window affects different parts of the room in the painting. This is something for which Vermeer is famous.

Delft is one of the Netherlands' biggest cities. For centuries, it has been famous for its white and blue pottery. Pottery is pots, bowls, and other objects that are made of clay. *Inset:* This picture is thought to have been painted by Vermeer of himself.

Young Vermeer

Jan Vermeer was born in 1632, in Delft, the Netherlands. His father, Reynier, owned an inn, or a small hotel. He also bought and sold artwork. It is believed that Vermeer became interested in art from being around his father's business as a child.

Before the seventeenth century, most artists painted scenes from history or pictures of rich families. During the Dutch Golden Age, artists began painting all kinds of subjects. People liked these new paintings and many had enough money to buy them for their homes or offices.

Learning How to Paint

Vermeer took over his family's art business after his father died, in 1652. In 1653, he joined the St. Luke's Guild. The guild was an **organization** for people who wanted to learn how to paint. Painting was not thought of as an art form at this time. It was seen as a way to make a living. Artists were asked by wealthy people to make the paintings that they wanted.

It was through the guild that Vermeer received his art training. It is thought that his six years of study were spent under a master painter, who taught Vermeer all about the painting trade.

Of Vermeer's own works, *The Art of Painting*, from around 1666, is thought to be the one he liked best. He never sold it, even when he needed money to pay his bills. The painter in the picture is believed to be Vermeer.

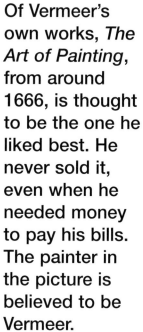

Church and Family Life

In 1653, Vermeer married Catherine Bolnes. She came from a wealthy **Catholic** family. Vermeer had been raised as a **Protestant**, but he **converted** to Catholicism when he married Catherine. At that time, most of the people in the Netherlands were Protestant, and they did not like Catholics.

Vermeer and Catherine moved in with her mother, Maria Thins. Thins had a house in the area of Delft where most of the Catholic families lived. She had enough money to help **support** Vermeer and his family, which over the years grew to 14 children.

Vermeer painted *The Allegory of the Faith* around 1670. "Allegory" means "to show an idea using pictures." In this painting, Vermeer uses the objects in the room to show ideas about the Catholic faith.

Top: Young Lady Seated at a Virginal, from around 1672, shows how Vermeer used pointillé to bring out the areas of bright sunlight.

Bottom: This is a camera obscura.

Pages 14–15: View of Delft, from around 1661, shows Vermeer's mastery of perspective in painting a realistic landscape.

Vermeer's Painting Techniques

In the 1650s, Vermeer began to paint scenes using a **technique** called pointillé. To do pointillé, Vermeer applied **layers** of small beads of paint to an object, which makes it appear brighter. He used this method to show how sunlight through a window makes the colors of certain objects stand out.

Many people believed that Vermeer used a camera obscura to draw the shapes of his subjects on a **canvas**. A camera obscura is a box with a lens in it. It can **project** a scene onto another surface, such as paper or a wall. This method helps an artist show realistic **perspective** in his or her paintings.

14

15

Success in Delft

Vermeer was respected among the artists of Delft. He was picked twice to be the leader of St. Luke's Guild. The people of Delft also liked Vermeer's paintings. His work was not known outside of Delft because he did not sell many of his paintings outside of the city.

Around this time, collecting paintings was becoming a more common hobby. Many artists did not charge much money for their work. This made it easy for more people to buy paintings to hang in their homes. Before the Dutch Golden Age, only rich people had enough money to buy paintings.

Young Woman with a Water Jug, from around 1662, is one of Vermeer's most famous paintings. It is one of his best studies of the effect light has on objects. For example, you can see how the light passes through the cloth on the woman's head.

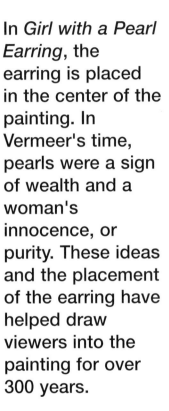

In *Girl with a Pearl Earring*, the earring is placed in the center of the painting. In Vermeer's time, pearls were a sign of wealth and a woman's innocence, or purity. These ideas and the placement of the earring have helped draw viewers into the painting for over 300 years.

Girl with a Pearl Earring

One of Vermeer's most famous paintings is called *Girl with a Pearl Earring*. It was painted around 1666. The painting is a mystery because no one knows who the girl is. No one knows either where Vermeer got the idea for the **turban** on her head. It is not like anything that Dutch women wore.

Vermeer makes us look at the pearl earring the girl is wearing by showing how it shines. To get this result, he used thick beads of white paint to show the part of the earring where light would hit it. This painting is now thought of as one of the greatest examples of Dutch Golden Age painting.

Money Troubles

In the early 1670s, France **invaded** the Netherlands. During this time, many Dutch businesses lost money. People no longer had enough money to buy paintings. This hurt Vermeer's painting and art-dealing businesses. Vermeer had to borrow money to pay his bills.

Vermeer worried so much about his money troubles that he got sick and could not paint. In December 1675, Vermeer died. He was outlived by Catherine and 11 of their children. He left behind a lot of bills that needed to be paid. To pay these bills, Catherine had to sell some of his paintings.

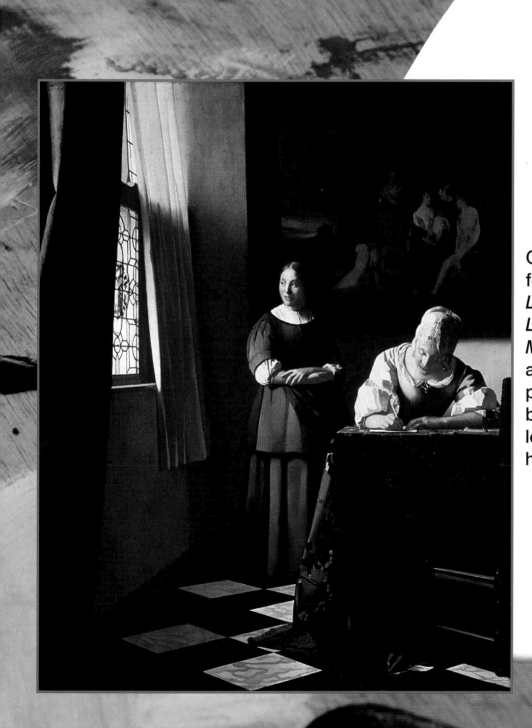

Catherine was forced to sell *Lady Writing a Letter with Her Maid*, painted around 1670, to pay some of the bills Vermeer left behind when he died.

Fame Comes Late

Vermeer was one of the greatest painters of the seventeenth century. Although he was respected in Delft, his paintings were not seen as great art. He did not become famous until almost 200 years after his death. In 1866, a man called Thoré-Bürger wrote about Vermeer's work. This caused people to take an interest in it.

During his life, Vermeer made only 35 paintings. He is known as a master at showing how rays of sunlight change the colors in a painting. Today, many of his works hang in **museums** around the world.

GLOSSARY

affects (uh-FEKTS) Changes.

canvas (KAN-ves) A cloth surface that is used for a painting.

Catholic (KATH-lik) Having to do with the Roman Catholic church.

converted (kun-VERT-ed) Changed from one faith to another.

invaded (in-VAYD-ed) Entered a place to take it over.

layers (LAY-erz) Coats or coatings of something.

museums (myoo-ZEE-umz) Places where art or historical pieces are safely kept for people to see and to study.

organization (or-guh-nuh-ZAY-shun) A group.

perspective (per-SPEK-tiv) Point of view.

project (pruh-JEKT) To show pictures of things on surfaces such as screens or paper.

Protestant (PRAH-tes-tunt) A Christian who does not belong to the Roman Catholic faith.

support (suh-PORT) To give money or necessities.

technique (tek-NEEK) A way of doing something.

turban (TUR-bun) A headdress made of a cloth that wraps around the head.

INDEX

WEB SITES

Due to the changing nature of Internet links, PowerKids Press has developed an online list of Web sites related to the subject of this book. This site is updated regularly. Please use this link to access the list:

www.powerkidslinks.com/mta/verm/